CORRODIES IN THE ENGLISH MONASTERIES

A STUDY IN ENGLISH SOCIAL HISTORY OF
THE MIDDLE AGES

A THESIS

IN MEDIEVAL HISTORY

PRESENTED TO THE FACULTY OF THE GRADUATE SCHOOL OF THE
UNIVERSITY OF PENNSYLVANIA IN PARTIAL FULFILLMENT
OF THE REQUIREMENTS FOR THE DEGREE
OF DOCTOR OF PHILOSOPHY

HOWARD MORRIS STUCKERT

WIPF & STOCK · Eugene, Oregon

Wipf and Stock Publishers
199 W 8th Ave, Suite 3
Eugene, OR 97401

Corrodies in the English Monasteries
A Study in English Social History of the Middle Ages
By Stuckert, Howard Morris
ISBN 13: 978-1-5326-7801-1
Publication date 12/21/2018
Previously published by University of Pennsylvania, 1923

ACKNOWLEDGMENT

This study has been prepared under the supervision of Professor Arthur C. Howland. I wish to acknowledge his many kind suggestions and helpful criticisms. Professor Edward P. Cheyney, whose precept and example have been a constant inspiration to me, has made many valuable suggestions for which I am grateful. Professor Roland C. Kent of the University of Pennsylvania and Professor Leonard Bloomfield of the Ohio State University have given me much needed help in philological matters.

CONTENTS

	PAGE
Chapter I. The Meaning of Corrody....................................	7

The word, its spelling, derivation and meanings — the monastic corrody, its kinds and definition.

Chapter II. The Origin of the Monastic Corrody................... 12

Four possible hypotheses — examination of the evidence for each — conclusion.

Chapter III. The Variety and Extent of Corrodies................. 17

Several classes of recipients of corrodies — corrodiers by purchase — corrodies demanded by king and nobility — geographical and chronological distribution.

Chapter IV. The Corrody as a Factor in the Medieval Economy.... 26

Content, value and variety of corrodies — their function in the Middle Ages as organized charity, old age pensions and annuity insurance.

Chapter V. The Corrody as a Form of Property..................... 30

It is negotiable, assignable and sometimes heritable — often converted into a money payment — its legal status as a form of real property — influence of actions for corrodies on the growth of the idea of incorporeal rights and incorporeal things — legal processes connected with corrodies.

Chapter VI. Abuses of the System and Efforts at Reform.......... 35

Extortionate practices of the king — abuses of corrodies by abbots — the corrody as disguised simony — the abuse of corrodies as a side light on medieval society — restrictions and prohibitions of popes, bishops, abbots, nobles and king.

Chapter VII. Corrodies as a Factor in Monastic Decline........... 44

Evil effect of corrody system on monastic discipline — a cause for increase of church property — mortgaging the future — recognition of the evil by king and clergy — the end of corrodies in the 16th century.

Appendix   I. Cognates and Derivatives of Conredum............ 50

Appendix II. Writs of Corrody..................................... 51

Appendix III. References to Literature............................ 52

CHAPTER I. THE MEANING OF CORRODY

The word corrody is found spelt in fifteen different forms. These may be classified to show the general course of their development, as follows: — con-redum, is the oldest form, from which was derived conredium. By the broadening of the vowel, conradium was later attained and at a still later date the form corrodium. The forms corredum, correda, corredium and corradium were naturally evolved from the preceding by assimilation of the "n" to the following "r". In certain regions of Central Europe "g" was substituted for "d" due probably to the pronunciation which the word received in those places. (Italy and Italian influence in Germany). This gives the series conregium, conragium and corragium. Another group was formed by the entire omission of the "d", viz: — conreius, conreium, correium and coureium.

Con-redum is a very old medieval word. It is a compound of the Latin con, with the force of cum and a Germanic word that was written in Latin as redum, having the probable meaning of apparatus or gear. Possibly the con or cum is the translation of a prefixed ge — as a Latin preposition was often used to translate the force of the German prefix. Cum gives the idea of compacted together and accentuates the idea of readiness.

The possible connotations of the root word, redum, are indicated in its existing cognates, a simple comparison of which reveals the common idea underlying all these words. Before our Germanic forefathers set out on a raid, they had to get ready, make preparations, equip themselves, rig up the harness on the horses or if the expedition was by sea, rig up the tackling of the ships. The idea of provision or preparation for a journey, the disposing and arranging things before locomotion is the fundamental conception, from which all the particular meanings of the word are readily derived. Corredare was to fit out and the corredum was the outfit, the provisions for the trip. In its most generalized sense, conredum meant arrangement, preparation, outfit, but the idea of motion or locomotion was never lost from it, just as "fertig" — ready, in German, is cognate to "fahren" — to go.[1]

The derivatives of conredum form an equally interesting series and retain the idea of locomotion that was so persistent in the older cognate words.

In the Middle Ages, the word corrody was used in a much more general sense than that of an annuity of food, clothing, shelter, etc., granted by a monastic house for a money consideration or at the request of king or noble. It may help to determine the origin of this institution, which is the real thing of interest to us, to consider the more general meaning of the word. Its most general connotation is that of any kind of supply, equipment or provision. This meaning is found wholly independent of monastic associations, as in the daily corrodies to be supplied the workmen who repaired and built up London after the great fire of the early thirteenth century.[2] Among the regulations of the Council, it was stipulated that carpenters were to receive 3d. and a corrody per diem or 4½d. without corrody. Plasterers and tilers were to receive the same but their helpers only half pence with a corrody or 3d. for all. Similar provision is made for stone masons and others. The money paid in substitution for the corrody was called "mete-silver".[3]

In Henry of Huntington,[4] the word is used for the equivalent of one meal, a banquet. The same meaning should be attached to the use of the word in the Laws of King Ethelred, (VIII. 2. A. D. 978 — 1016.) [5] Both of these are twelfth century documents that embody older material.

An entirely different meaning is found for the use of the word in certain twelfth century writs of Henry I., Stephen and Rich-

---

[1] For linguistic information, I am much indebted to Professor Roland G. Kent of the University of Pennsylvania and Professor Leonard Bloomfield of the Ohio State University. "Murray" and the elymological dictionaries of Skeat and Weekley should be consulted, also Kluge, F., Etymologisches Wörterbuch der deutsher Sprache and Scheler, A., Dictionairre d'etymologie francaise. See Appendix for Cognates and Derivatives.

[2] Liber Custumarum London 1212 in Munimenta Gildhallæ Londoniensis (R. S. vol. 12, pt. 2, I. p. 86.)

[3] ib. pt. 2, II. p. 791.

[4] History of the English, by Henry Archdeacon of Huntingdon (R. S. vol. 74, p. 197.)

[5] Liebermann vol. I, p. 260 and Thorpe vol. I, p. 337.

ard I., viz. "Writ of King Henry to Warin, provost of Hampton and his assistants: — I enjoin that you return quickly whatever you have taken from the proper corrody (de proprio corredio) of the Abbot of Abington by toll or custom and henceforth you shall take nothing by toll or custom from his corrody, or from the things which his men are able to swear are his property." Here the word is used in the most general sense, of equipment and provisions or supplies.[6]

The same broad significance is to be given in the following reference to Borough customs. At Coventry (1181) under limitation of the lord's credit, we read "And furthermore, together with the other privileges, that the said burgesses shall not lend the said earl or his men anything in corrody" (as provision, maintenance or outfit) "or otherwise, save on condition that they are secure of the return of their chattel."[7] The meaning is tolerably clear. To lend in corrody, is to lend some property as an equipment or provision for some necessity, possibly oxen for plowing. The townspeople were assured of the return of their provision. Compare with this the similar use of the word, in the very old reference in the Testament of Protasius, who was Archdeacon of Urgel, Catalonia and Abbot of Exalata, (Cuxan) in the year 878, quoted in Ducange,[8] where an enumeration of the cattle, sheep, horses, swine, monk's vestments, iron instruments, etc., of the monastry is presented to the lord as the conredum of his monastery.

"Corrody" was used in a still different and more particular sense, apparently in Italy, for the equipment and rigging of ships. (Contract of navy of St. Louis with Venice.[9] By a curious extension of meaning, it was applied to the rigging of women, their trousseaux.

In a charter of Louis VII., 1157, granted to the Church of Notre Dame of Paris, conferring immunity upon certain of its

---
[6] Chronicon Monasterii de Abingdon, (R. S. vol. 2, pt. 2, pp. 80, 182, 183.) Charter Rolls vol. II, p. 81, Vol. V, p. 160. Calendar of Documents Preserved in France, vol. I, p. 98.
[7] Seldon Sy. vol. 21, (1906) Borough Customs vol. II., p. 86. Confirmed by Henry III., Charter Rolls, vol. II., p. 88, (1268.)
[8] Ducange II, 545, s. v. correda et corredum.
[9] Ducange II, 545, s. v. conredum.

towns, he particularly stipulates that there shall not be exacted by him or his successors or his servants, a certain convivia which in common speech is called "corredae" or "gistae".[10] Here "corrody" is taken to be the same as the gestum or gite — a feudal custom whereby the seigneur had the right to be entertained, he and his suite, by his vassal when he passed through the vassal's land.[11]

The word thus has many meanings beside that of provision supplied by a monastery and all are developed from the most general notion of provision or equipment.

The word corrody (Lat. conredum) meant any kind of supply or provisioning and was so used in this general comprehensive sense from at least 800 A. D. onward for three hundred years before it was applied to a special kind of provisioning by monastic houses. After 1100, the sources repeatedly refer to corrodies as a specific monastic institution which appears fully developed in England by that time. Indeed when we first have clear references to it, abuses have already sprung up in its administration and the institution is in need of reform and regulation.

The monastic houses of the 12th and 13th centuries in England, were providing corrodies for four quite distinct classes of persons.

1. The monks and nuns themselves were legally entitled to a definite amount of provision in food, clothing and shelter. This was the monk's corrody.

2. Provision of various kinds was granted to the servants and friends of a monastery, who were in no way bound by monastic vows. A considerable group of agents to attend to the secular business of the monasteries was thus provided for and their provision was also called a corrody.

3. Another extensive group were the "corrodiers by purchase". These, by paying a certain sum of money or by deeding their real estate to the monastery, were given a comfortable living for the balance of their lives. This class included unmarried women, widows, widowers and old couples.

---

[10] Documents inédits, vol. 15, pt. 1. Cartulaire de l'Eglise Notre Dame de Paris, p. 271.

[11] Documents inédits, vol. 1 of Cartulaire de l'abbaye de Saint-pere de Chartres, p. CXLIX.

4. There still remained a fourth class, whose corrody or provision was exacted from the monastery by king or nobility. This class, while smaller in number attracted the most attention because of the official and legal relations of king or noble to the monastic house and because the living so exacted amounted to a complete loss to the monastery.

These four types of corrody, while differing as to their recipients and as to the manner of granting and their purpose, had certain features in common. They were clearly distinguishable from pensions or annual payments in money, although such pensions were sometimes attached to the corrodies. Again while land and sometimes very extensive grants of property accompanied a corrody, these were not only unusual, but not characteristic of the corrody. The corrody necessarily included provisions of food, clothing and shelter. Further it was granted by a religious community. These conditions being fulfilled, the corrodies varied endlessly not only as to content but also as to their recipients and as to the manner in which they were granted.

The monastic corrody may then be defined as a specified allowance of food and drink with the use of room or rooms and other privoleges granted by a monastery to a person or couple with or without servant, 1) in consideration for a money payment or a grant of property to the monastery; 2) upon the demand of king or noble; 3) in payment for services of various sorts rendered to the monastery. The interest in corrodies as a medieval monastic institution centers in the corrodies that were purchased and those demanded by the nobility and king. These will receive special consideration.

CHAPTER II. THE ORIGIN OF THE MONASTIC CORRODY

Our knowledge of the origin of the monastic corrody is hypothetical owing to the fact that the sources of information are limited to a few isolated texts of uncertain interpretation. Four possible solutions of the problem of origin might be suggested. (1) The corrody system may have grown out of the right of purveyance, the right of the lord to require his vassal to entertain him and his entourage when traveling or hunting. This in French, was called the "gite". The claim to sustenance was — according to this theory — commuted by the monastery into a certain annual provision which was transferable to another. (2) The corrody may have been originally a kind of feudal rental or relief. A founder or donor of a monastery, when granting the land, may have reserved for himself and his heirs a right of maintenance in the monastic house. This would lead to the corrody system as soon as the donor appointed another than himself to receive the maintenance. (3) Again it is quite possible that the custom of granting corrodies began as a provision for the dispossessed relatives of the founder of a monastery. Having deprived his relatives of the right to inherit the land which was given to the monastery, the donor compensates them by reserving a right of annual provision for their benefit. (4) Hospitality thoroughly characterized monastic life. Nothing was easier than for the neighboring lord to impose upon the monastery in this matter, until he developed a kind of prescriptive right to demand sustenance for himself or one who represented him.

What evidence is there for any of these possible solutions? The evidence of etymology and semantics is precarious, but words frequently are "fossilized" institutions. The one conclusion that is indisputable from the study of the word conredum in the preceding chapter, is that it connotes provisioning for a journey. That "conredum" as used in the earlier Middle Ages means harnessing or rigging for a journey is beyond doubt.

This would suggest the first hypothesis that the monastic corrody in its earliest form was practically identical with the lord's right of maintenance when travelling through the land of his vassals. It was a right that grew up out of the peculiar relationship of dependence of the vassal on the lord in the feudal system. The founder of a monastic house granted the lands for its support and the house in many cases held its land as a vassal of the founder or his successors. Even where the land was held in "frank almoigne", the right of patronage or advowson was reserved. It was only natural that the patrons and donors and their heirs should be given the hospitality of the monastery at all times. This explanation identifies the corrody with the gite or gesta or what was elsewhere called procuratio or herbergamentum.[12] We actually have in the charter of Louis VII. (1157) above cited, the identification of the "gite" and the corrody,[13] "convivia que vulgo corredae vel gistae vocantur." From this it seems quite probable that the corrody was originally a simpler affair, a temporary matter rather than a permanent maintenance. The right to it was doubtless permanent but was only occasionally exercised (as once a year) by the lord and from this grew into a right of continual provisioning and then one which could be turned over to one's representative.

In support of the second hypothesis, that the corrody grew out of a feudal rent or relief, we have a curious passage in chapter 70 of the Laws of Ine (A. D. 688-725). This was translated into Latin at a much later date, during the Norman French period. Here the word corrody was used to translate the old English "foster" — a portion of sustenance to be provided by a vassal for his lord.[14] "With ten hides, as 'foster', ten vessels of honey, three hundrd loaves, twelve 'ambers' of "Wilisc' ale, thirty of clear, two full-yeared oxen or ten wethers, ten geese, twenty hens, ten cheeses, an 'amber' full of butter, five salmon, twenty pounds of fodder and one hundred eels." That is, for those holding as much as ten hides of land, a maintenance of all these things was to be paid back to the lord as an annual

---

[12] See note 11.
[13] See note 10.
[14] Liebermann I, p. 119. Thorpe vol. I, p. 147. vol. II, p. 471.

rental. This was translated as follows in the Latin: decem hidis ad corredium debent reddi X dolia mellis, ccc panes, etc. Lieberman translates this into modern German, "zum Unterhalt (als Jahreszins)."

If this is the true explanation it might be expected that the charters of foundation would indicate it in some way. But in no instance do we find a foundation charter — and they are legion — making any provision for a corrody. The nearest approach to it is a charter of Henry I. founding the Hospital of St. Leonard, York, where he says "These we grant for the salvation of our souls, etc., and that we be participants in all the goods which may be in your holy house, in life and in death." The general absence of such claims in foundation charters does not go to prove that they were not made. It was quite natural that they should be made without any written agreement in the matter, and maintained through many generations by the heirs of founders and donors. It is further conceivable that this right of entertainment was extended from the occasional enjoyment of the hospitality of the house to a claim to the right of continuous and life-long maintenance. In time this was delegated to an attorney. In brief, a feudal right of occasional entertainment may have developed into a legal right for the heirs of patrons and donors to impose the grant of a permanent living.

This view comes nearest to the traditional medieval explanation of the origin of the corrody. The patronage of a monstery was often vested in the king because he or one of his predecessors had founded the house. In 1364 Edward III. claimed a corrody in St. Albans by reason of his right of patronage, "ratione patronatus", but released the house from it because of a grant of lands to him by the monastery. In the indenture the claim is based on the fact that "the said Abbey . . . is of the foundation of the progenitors of our said Lord the King and of his own patronage." But the foundation of St. Albans had taken place in the dim past of the early Saxon kings, centuries before. There is nothing that would lead us to believe, and in itself it seems intrinsically unlikely, that the kings had been appointing corrodiers through all those centuries. In fact the monks of St. Albans insisted that a corrody had never been granted to any secular authority before the time of Edward I. and then not at the instance of the king but of Earl Edmund, son of Henry III. They were then forced to grant a corrody to one of the Earl's family and "from this time the king began to exact a corrody."

Whether the monks of St. Albans were right or wrong in the facts, corrodies were demanded and granted and bought and sold elsewhere from at least the year 1100 on.[15] The right to reserve corrody or maintenance had been quitclaimed in many places, but was doubtless revived after 1100 and also imposed in many places where it had never before existed. The old custom provided a legal justification for the exactions of royalty and others. In the sixteenth century the idea was very widespread that corrodies sprang from the legal right of donors, who were not necessarily founders.[16] We can readily see how this developed out of the tradition of the Middle Ages.

There is no evidence that the corrody originated as an abuse of monastic hospitality, although that was quite possible, and such abuse certainly is reflected in the Statutes of 3 Edward I. and 2 Edward II. and contributed to the general monastic decline of that period.[17] There is also no evidence that the corrody originated as a device to provide for dispossessed relatives of founders, although that was occasionally done. Henry de Bagenore gave to the convent of Poghel all his land of Bagenore, etc., for which among other things the canons found *for all his children* a fitting maintenance (garisonem).[18]

Two other significant cases remain to be considered. Both are Norman French. In both the claim to corrody or provision was inherited. In both the corrody was part and parcel of a feudal relationship and right and finally it was not a living that was received week by week, day by day, but a right of maintenance that was more occasional.

A charter of 1218 at Mont S. Michel reads: "I Ruelendus Goion, by the wish of Robert Goion, my first begotten brother,

---

[15] Chronica Monasterii, S. Albani, Rolls Series, vol. 28, pt. 7, pp. 113, 100, 394.
[16] Savine: English Monasteries, etc., p. 242.
[17] Statutes of the Realm, vol. I, pp. 26, 153. (1275, 1309).
[18] Calendar of Charter Rolls, vol. IV, p. 125. (1329).

have released to the Abbot and convent of St. Michael whatever conredum that was contained in the portion which came to me from my paternal inheritance, what namely I was accustomed to receive in the abbey annually."[19]

In the Calendar of Documents preserved in France, are two charters relating to an interesting and early case. Early in the twelfth century Walter Giffard, Earl of Buckingham, confirmed to the priory of Longueville all that he and his parents had given them and further renounced his right to a corrody (procurationis) due him at Witchinghame in England. From this we infer that previous to this time the Earl of Buckingham had the right to go to Witchinghame and enjoy the hospitality of the monks of that cell whenever he wished. A charter of Henry II. (1155) confirming the above states "the monks to be free of the corrody which Walter had reserved to himself there and which his son quitclaimed afterward." [20]

To sum up in conclusion: the origin of the corrody remains quite hypothetical for the reason that our records are scanty, precisely where they should be full. Certain inferences seem justifiable. Although the word corrody is much older, the corrody system as a monastic institution probably developed in Normandy in the eleventh and possibly in the tenth century. From there it naturally was transferred to England. It probably developed out of the feudal relationship of monasteries to their founders, donors and patrons. This relationship expressed itself either as the right of purveyance or as some form of relief or as both. This cannot be determined. Then the right of entertainment grew into the corrody system, which was an imposition and a burden on the good-will and resources of the monasteries.[21]

---

[19] Ducange, vol. II, p. 545, s. v. conredium.

[20] Calendar of Documents Preserved in France, vol. I, pp. 75, 77.

[21] The explanation of the origin of corrodies in Stephen's Commentary is wholly unhistorical. In vol. II., p. 721, note K, he says, "The King, in imitation of Emperor of Germany, exercised (or claimed to exercise), the right of naming to the first prebend that became vacant after his accession, and this prerogative probably gave rise to corrodies, viz.: — the right (now disused) of the King to send one of the royal chaplains to be maintained by the Bishop, or to have a pension allowed him till the Bishop promoted him to a benefice."

CHAPTER III. VARIETY AND EXTENT OF CORRODEIS

The simplest form of corrody was the portion of food and clothing which was the monk's own, as of right, his peculium. After his death the provision was kept separate and continued for a whole year. "On the day of the death of a monk, the servants of the infirmary shall have the whole of his corrody. Afterward for a whole year his corrody shall be given to whomever the prior assigns it." [22] The grant of a corrody was made to a visiting monk of the same congregation (commonachi) during his stay at the Abbey.[23] Corrodies were also granted to retired abbots and priors, although these in many cases seemed to have difficulty in maintaining their claims to a full corrody after the lapse of time, with the result that pope or king interfered in their favor.[24]

Another kind of corrody extending beyond those who were under monastic vows, consisted in grants made to chaplains and vicars. The Hospital of St. John Baptist at Brugg, diocese of Bath and Wells, gave to the Chaplains of St. Mary's, Wolavynpton, as a corrody 33s, 4d. yearly and eight quarters of good clean corn of eight bushels each, with right of recovery by writ of novel disseisin.[25] Similarly a corrody went with the Chaplaincy of All Saints, Little Cranford, granted by the Abbey of Tarent in consideration of the sum of £20. On the other hand, the Parson of Kydesford paid £200 to the Convent of Stoke Curcy for his corrody but the provision was added that if sick or absent, he should receive instead 2s. per week and "a meal and night's lodging for a friend once or twice a month without paying for it." [26] A good illustration of the way the corrody was extended outside of the monastic house itself is found in

---
[22] 13 Century Register, Priory of Worcester, Camden Sy. vol. 91, p. 131a; Also Constitutions and Custumal of Evesham (1214) Rolls Series, vol. 29, p. 220; in Dugdale, vol. II., p. 31; Historia Abingdon (1154), Rolls Series, vol. 2, p. 237 ff.
[23] Chronicle of Evesham (1317) Rolls Series, vol. 29, p. 291.
[24] Patent Rolls, 1352, p. 255. Papal Letters X, 591. Papal Register IV, 374.
[25] Papal Registers IV, 279 also 276.
[26] Patent Rolls, 1381, p. 29 and 1383, p. 221.

the case of John Kyneton, who granted in the time of Edward III, certain land and rents to the convent of Roche for a secular chaplain for a chapel of the Holy Trinity at Kyneton. The convent was to find the chaplain and provide his corrody. Henry IV. in 1401 gave license to the Abbey to grant the said land to the chaplain in mortmain in exchange for the corrody. Evidently the monastery had come to feel that the corrody was a burden and was willing to lose the land in order to be quit of the corrody.[27]

Another type of corrody still further removed from the inner circle of the convent is that conferred upon *servants and friends* of the monastery. Every official and servant in the monastery, even down to the "cookie" who turned the cakes, received his corrody.[28] The Consuetudines of the Abbey of Abingdon (1154-1189) make provision for each officer and servant and in some instances the provision is referred to as a corrody. When the Abbey of Croyland was in the hands of the kings escheator, during a vacancy in the office of abbot (1310), there were forty-one monks and no novices, and the corrodiers were as follows:— five chaplains and ten others, who under seal of the house, received a monk's corrody, i. e. daily, one loaf, one and a half gallons of ale and two plates from the kitchen; while a certain Thomas de Hakebech received a full corrody for secretarial work. Others received a lesser corrody, viz. the servant in the church, two caretakers in the infirmary, a servant in the monks' refectory, a hostler, a servant in the common hall, a cook in the community kitchen, a cook in the infirmary kitchen, a buyer of meat, fish, etc., two servants in the cellar, two bakers, two brewers, two servants in the sleeping hall, a servant in the granary, two millers for a horse-mill and a wind-mill, a janitor, a cobbler, a tailor, a wash-room attendant, a servant in the almshouse to collect and distribute alms, a carpenter, a cement worker, a plumber, a plasterer, an iron-worker, a wagoner and four stablemen. These fifty-one corrodiers, as well as the watchman, marshal and forrester, were ignored by the escheator during the va-

---

[27] Patent Rolls 1401, p. 507.
[28] Dugdale III., p. 43. Chronicon Monasterii de Abingdon, Rolls Series, vol. 2, pt. 2, pp. 237, 241, 300. Dugdale vol. II, p. 121.

cancy, to their great distress. This description which presents us with a rather lively picture of the manifold activities of a monastic community, shows how each servant was assigned his own proper maintenance according to his station. The corrody in these cases is practically the equivalent of wages for services rendered to the monastery.

Other instances of similar corrodies follow. When tenants of an abbey worked the lands of the lord Abbot, they were provided with a corrody on the days of their service.[29] Even the swineheard received a liberal corrody for himself and his wife.[30] A waiter on the table at St. Paul's London, received a corrody and one half penny in payment for his services.[31] The Knights Hospitallers of England in 1338, numbered one hundred nineteen brethren, three lay brethren (donati) and eighty corrodiers, serving the order in varied capacities.[32] Even an organist received a corrody with five marks per annum and firewood and undertook therefor to play "at the mass of the Blessed Virgin and at high-mass on Festival days, at the vigils if there be any singing, at chapter and at vespers unless he shall have leave or be ill or detained by any other great reason, and that he shall teach four boys and one monk to play on the organ (plusare organa) and any other monk who may wish to apply himself to such study."[33] Three times within one decade (1349 and 1358) Christ Church Canterbury conferred corrodies upon lawyers for their advice and assistance -- in the first instance to Richard Vachan, LL. D., the Archdeacon of Surrey, and again to a Thomas Mason and to John Eccleshole, Canon of London. Beside food and clothing, the first of these received for life the use of a room and squire, three servants and three houses with equipment and maintenance within the convent. It is not told whether counsel exacted this fee or whether the monks of Canterbury were so pleased with his advice upon the death of Arch-

---

[29] Cartulary of the Abbey of Ramsey, Rolls Series, vol. 79, pt. 3, pp. 245, 293. Rental and Custumal of Glastonbury, Somerset Sy, vol. 5, p. 205.
[30] Cartularium Abbathiae de Rievalle, Surtees Sy., vol. 83, p. 355.
[31] Domesday of St. Pauls, Camden Sy. Vol. 69, p. 29 and LXXII.
[32] Knights Hospitallers in England, Camden Sy. Vol. 65, p. 214.
[33] Two Cartularies of the Benedictine Abbeys of Muchelney and Athelney, Somerset Record Sy. Vol. 14, p. 24.

bishop Stratford[34] that they did not look upon the payment as exorbitant. Others who came to the rescue of the monastery with force or other substantial assistance, were also granted corrodies,[35] as in the case of William de la Marche who came to the aid of St. Albans against their rebellious tenants.

Collegiate Churches also were grantors in favor of their canons and vicars,[36] and probably others. The Collegiate Church being much like a monastic institution it was natural that the monastic corrody should be found there also.

The temptation to grant a corrody for a money consideration was too great to be resisted. So all over England the custom grew up of *selling* corrodies for cash or of granting them in return for a piece of property transferred to the monastery. The convent of Melsa, a house of the Cistercian Order, under William of Dringhow (1349-53) raised £500, the equivalent of five-sixths of a year's income by the sale of corrodies.[37] In 1396 at the same monastery there were fifteen corrodiers. Abbot Hugh of St. Alban's died (1326) leaving that monastery 5000 marks in debt. The corrodiers had increased to over fifty-four and he had raised over £1000 by the sale of corrodies.[38] Glastonbury in 1189 had twenty-one corrodiers one of whom had ben appointed by the crown, others by escheaters and some by the abbots. Selby Abbey in 1342 had eleven corrodies owing to eleven persons, one of whom also had provision for a servant and a horse.[39] In the Book of the Benefactors of St. Albans, it is noted that Bartholomew of Wendover, rector of the church of Shakrestone, gave 240 marks for a corrody "not too burdensome, but very excellent." This extraordinary price he paid in order to hasten the work of building.[40] In the time of Edward II the Wardens of London Bridge and the brethren of the Bridge House gave to Henry-in-

---

[34] Letter Books of the Monastery of Christ Church Canterbury, Rolls Series, vol. 85, pt. 2, pp. 290, 293, 354 and 370.

[35] Chronica Monasterii de Melsa, Rolls Series, vol. 43, pt. 3, p. 4 and Chronica Monasterii S. Albani, Rolls Series, vol. 28, pt. 7, pp. 100 and 394.

[36] Calendar of Papal Registers, vol. I, p. 280.

[37] Chronica Monasterii de Melsa, Rolls Series, Vol. 43, pt. 3, pp. XIII and LXVII.

[38] Chronica Monasterii S. Albani, Rolls Series, vol. 28, pt. 6, p. 178.

[39] Rentalia et Custumaria Monasterii Glastoniae, Somerset Record Sy., vol. 5, p. XXIII., Coucher Books of Selby, Yorkshire Archaeological Society, Record Series, vol. 13, pp. 304 f.

[40] Chronica Monasterii S. Albani, Rolls Series, vol. 28, pt. 4, p. 454.

the-Lane and his wife two corrodies for a consideration of 100 marks sterling. This provided also for the maintenance of a servant and for two rooms. As the corrodiers had to give a year's notice if they wished to relinquish their rooms, these must have been of economic value.[41] Other corrodies were sold for smaller sums — 50 marks, £60 and even £20 and in some instances the consideration is not mentioned, or dismissed as a "certain sum paid down."[42] In such cases it was probably not much, but the religious houses were in need. The Priory of St. Frideswide, Oxford, sold a corrody for a man and his groom for £100. But they broke up his room, doubtless a frame structure, and carried away his goods together with the "writing which he had for the corrody."[43]

Many of the charters issued by monasteries when granting this kind of corrody were "inspected" and confirmed by the king and at one time at least the king took the position that corrodies could not be granted by a monastic house holding from him in chief, without his confirmation. Despite the frequent recurrence of confirmations, there undoubtedly were many corrodies granted of which the king never so much as heard. Bishops and local lords also claimed the same right of snupervision and confirmation, as we shall see in another connection.

So far only corrodies granted freely by the monastery to servants, officials and friends and those granted as a means of raising income, have been considered, but another kind although numerically fewer, has attracted more attention because it was felt to be an imposition and a burden. These were granted by the monastic house at the *request of king or bishop or some noble donor.*

Considering first those demanded by the clergy, we read of a corrody granted by the convent of Holy Trinity, London, in 1278, at the instance of the Bishop of London and enforced by the mandate of Pope Gregory X.[44] The Lord Bishop of Durham (1315), imposed on the Hospital of St. Giles at Kipiers,

---
[41] Munimenta Gildhallae Londoniensis, Rolls Series, vol. 12, pt. 3, pp. 449-453.
[42] Calendar of Patent Rolls, 1354, p. 28; 1360, pp. 364 and 428; 1340, p. 649.
[43] Calendar of Patent Rolls, 1318, p. 296.
[44] Calendar of Patent Rolls, 1414, p. 202, Calendar of Ancient Deeds, vol. V., A. 11956.

the granting of a corrody with 6s. 8d. annually, and other instances are found elsewhere.[45]

That many monastic houses were burdened by the inordinate demands of noblemen and other laity of less importance is seen in the first Statute of Westminster 1275, where it is said "Because that Abbeys and Houses of Religion of the land have been overcharged and sore grieved, by the resort of Great Men and other, so that their goods have not been sufficient for themselves, whereby they have been greatly hindered and impoverished, that thy cannot maintain themselves, nor such charity as they have been accustomed to do, It is Provided, that none shall come to eat or lodge in any house of religion of any other's Foundation than of his own, at the cost of the House, unless he be required (specially invited or requested) by the Governor of the house before his coming thither. And that none, at his own costs shall enter and come to lie there against the Will of them that be of the House. And by this Statute the King intendenth not that the Grace of Hospitality should be withdrawn from such as need; nor that the founders of such monasteries should overcharge or grieve them by their often coming."[46] This statute undoubtedly refers to the exaction of corrodies and was so understood in the Articuli Cleri (see page 42 below) and the later legislation. From this it is to be inferred that the practice of demanding sustenance by donors and others who were not founders and donors, had grown to dimensions that attracted attention and necessitated action and that even founders and the heirs of founders, were overburdening their foundations.

But the king was the chief offender in requiring the monasteries to grant livings to others than those interested in the immediate life and work of the monastery. During a vacancy at Ramsey in 1211, there were four corrodies, three of which were at the behest of the king.[47] The Close Rolls[48] reveal that Edward I demanded of different monasteries seven corrodies in 1293 and seven others in 1297. Edward III had even a worse

---

[45] Registrum Palatinum Dunelmense, Rolls Series, vol. 62, pt. 4, p. 411, and Oliver, Monasticon, p. 6. (St. German's Cornwall, by Bp. of Exeter, in Valor Eccl.)
[46] Statutes of the Realm, 3, Ed. I., vol. I, p. 26.
[47] Cartulary of the Abbey of Ramsey, Rolls Series, vol. 79, pt. 8, p. 215.
[48] Calendar of the Close Rolls, for years cited, see Indices.

record: — twenty-three in 1349, five in 1350, six in 1351, four in 1353, seven in 1354, six in 1355, six in 1356, ten in 1357, ten in 1358 and seven in 1359. Seventy-nine in one decade may not seem many but it is to be remembered that these were grants for life and that the Close Rolls do not give a complete list of such grants. This is shown by a comparison of the Close Rolls with the Patent Rolls and other documents. The king must have had his corrodiers scattered among the monastic houses, big and little throughout the length and breadth of the land. In the days of Henry VII the corrody system was such an important part of the king's income that the author of the "Italian Relation" says regarding it, "if the abbeys founded by the crown do not actually pay money to the king, they are obliged to defray the expenses of one, two or three gentlemen, and as many horses with their keep, at the pleasure of his Majesty. Because, whenever the king wishes to bestow an easy life upon one of his servants, he makes some one of these monasteries pay his expenses."[49] In 1535, according to the Valor Ecclesiasticus, the king had one or two corrodians in each of one hundred nineteen monasteries.[50]

Requests for support came frequently to the king and these were occasionally refused.[51] King's servants, old soldiers in the wars, favorites of the king, the king's aged surgeon and his watchman, among others, were given genial homes in the monasteries in which to spend their declining years.[52] Occasionally a corrody is imposed by way of punishment. One of the household of Edmund, the king's brother, was treated roughly by the servants of the abbey. By order of the king, at the instance of Edmund, a corrody for life is exacted from the abbey.[53] The queen frequently interested herself in the affairs of the religious

---

[49] Pollard, Reign of Henry VII., vol. II., p. 25, also Camden Sy. Publications, Series I, vol. 37.
[50] Savine, English Monasteries on the Eve of the Dissolution, p. 242. In Oxford Studies in Social and Legal History, vol. I.
[51] Records of Parliament, Rolls Series, Vol. 98, pp. 199, 200; Numbers 336 and 342 in Petitions of Scotland in Memoranda of Parliament (1305).
[52] Liber Benefactorum Ecclesiae Ramesiensis, Rolls Series, Vol. 83, pp. 281-385. (Ramsey 1303).
[53] Chronica Monasterii S. Albani, Rolls Series, Vol. 28, pt. 5, pp. 469, 484.

houses and the king often demanded a corrody as a favor to the queen or to provide for her servants.[54]

The king's claims were evidently based upon one or more of four distinct but related circumstances.[55] 1) Lands of the monastery held from the king, especially lands held in chief, i. e. directly. If only some of the lands of a monastery were held from the king, it seemed to establish the claim of the crown at least in its own opinion. 2) If the convent were of royal patronage or advowson, the king would appoint to a corrody. 3) If the monastery had been founded by a royal progenitor or predecessor, that provided another plausible ground for exacting a corrody. 4) Finally, the former granting of a corrody at the king's instance established a precedent, the king's solemn and repeated asseveration to the contrary. Nominations by the king were made to monasteries where some or none of these grounds existed and when the cases were taken into court, the decisions were usually against the king's right to appoint.[56]

As to the *distribution and extent* of corrodies, they seem to have been granted in every locality in England, although certain monasteries do not appear to have been burdened by them. In the diocese of Lincoln[57] as revealed by the subsidy collected in 1526, there were eighty-eight corrodiers of different sorts, distributed as follows:

---

[54] Calendar of Patent Rolls, 1347, p. 404. Camden Sy. Publications, Vol. 91, Registrum Prioratus Beatae Mariae Wigorniensis, pp. 175 ff.

[55] Advowson, the right of nominating a clergyman to a church or other ecclesiastical benefice such as an abbacy, was originally held by the founder of the church or monastery and inherited by his heirs. But as most churches were built as manor churches, the Lord of the Manor usually was the patron and so from this the custom in time grew up of appending the right of advowson to the manor in which the church was built. The advowson was legally a marketable right and could be transferred to another, either by deed or will, so that advowsons were sometimes transferred from land-owners to other private persons without land, or to ecclesiastical corporations. When thus severed from ownership of land, they are called advowsons in gross. Hence royal patronage or advowson could be acquired by the king quite independently of royal foundation or of the fact that the church or monastery held its land from the king directly or in chief.

[56] Calendar of Patent Rolls, 1340, p. 67; 1341, p. 293; 1346, p. 83; 1347, p. 404; 1353, p. 479.

[57] Subsidy Collected in Diocese of Lincoln, 1526, ed. H. Salter, Ox. 1909.

8 corrodies in 7 houses out of 19 in City of Lincoln.
21 corrodies in 9 houses out of 31 in Lincolnshire outside of City.
6 corrodies in 4 houses out of 12 in Leicestershire.
23 corrodies in 3 houses out of 16 in Northampton (Archdeaconry).
6 corrodies in 3 houses out of 8 in Huntingdon (Archdeaconry).
8 corrodies in 5 houses out of 11 in Bedford (Archdeaconry).
3 corrodies in 2 houses out of 10 in Buckingham (Archdeaconry).
13 corrodies in 6 houses out of 13 in Oxford (Archdeaconry).

Although the word corrody itself is very old, I have not found it used before the middle of the 12th century as the technical designation of the monastic corrody.[58] The sale of corrodies seems to be equally ancient (1139)[59], in fact their abuse already needed correction. In the Constitutions of Hubert, Archbishop of Canterbury, (1193-1205), it was enjoined that no corrody be granted without the common consent of the Abbey as a whole, i. e. the Abbot alone should not dispense corrodies.[60] The corrody as an institution right down to the dissolution of the monasteries under Henry VIII. (1539).

No pronounced development in the character or content of corrodies or in the conditions and circumstances of their granting, is noticeable in the four centuries from 1139 to 1539, during which we have full evidence concerning them. By comparison the later corrodies appear somewhat more ample in content and therefore more burdensome to the monastery than the earlier. Otherwise no development is apparent from an analysis of the available sources.

---

[58] Calendar of Documents Preserved in France, Vol. I, pp. 75, 76, 77. Calendar of Ancient Deeds, Vol. II, A 1888 cf. Dugdale Vol. VII, p. 609 and Vol. III, p. 43. Chronicon Monasterii de Abingdon, Rolls Series, Vol. 2, pt. 2, pp. 237, 241.
[59] Cartulary of St. John of Pontefract, Vol. I. Yorkshire Archaeological Sy., Vol. 25, p. 274 and Cartulary of St. John of Pontefract, Vol. II., Yorkshire Archaeological Sy., Vol. 30, p. 523. Rentalia et Custumaria Monasterii Glastoniae, Somerset Record Sy., Vol. 5, p. XXIII.
[60] Cartulary of the Abbey of Ramsey, Rolls Series, Vol. 79, pt. 2, pp. 198, 206 cf. Memorials of St. Edmund's Abbey, Rolls Series, Vol. 96, pt. 1, pp. 315 ff.

CHAPTER IV. THE CORRODY AS A FACTOR IN THE MEDIEVAL ECONOMY

The corrody is frequently spoken of as 1) a livery or living (liberatio), 2) an exhibition or tax (exhibitio) or 3) in a few cases as a procuration, a provision supplied by the vassal to the lord (procuratio). It is clearly distinguishable from a pension which is a sum of money granted annually without food, clothing or shelter and from a portion which is an assignment of land.[61]

The corrody consisted fundamentally of daily bread and ale, usually two loaves and two gallons, with one or two cooked plates or servings from the kitchen, for the two main meals.[62] Often several loads of firewood were supplied annually by the convent. The use of a room or suite of rooms was granted and often provision for a servant. An annual gown or robe was also frequently specified of such value or style as befitted the station of life of the corrodier. Sometimes candles and beer were to be supplied at night. Fodder for one or two horses with stalling might be included. Freedom of access to the room, ingress and egress, was frequently stipulated. In some instances land was granted with the corrody, or perhaps a tenement in the town was included.[63] Some corrodies provided in addition, a house with garden and pasturage for cattle and sheep and also a liberal pension.[64] In the fifteenth and sixteenth centuries, the grants seem to be fuller than those of earlier date. Complete equipment for housekeeping and farming was provided.[65] We incorporate two descriptions of later corrodies, taken from the Cartulary of the Cistercian Abbey of Rievaulx.[66]

---

[61] Dugdale, vol. II, p. 241.
[62] Letter Books of the Monastery of Christ Church Canterbury, Rolls Series, vol. 85, pt. 2, pp. 290, 293, 298, 334, 342, 370; pt. 3, p. 13; Cartulary of the Abbey of Ramsey, Rolls Series, vol. 79, pt. 2, p. 134.
[63] Registrum Malmesburiense, Rolls Series, vol. 72, pt. 2, p. 298.
[64] Calendar of Patent Rolls, 1343, p. 39; Calendar of Ancient Deeds, vol. III., D 1070.
[65] Cartularium Abbathiae de Rievalle, Surtees Sy., vol. 83, pp. 349, 355.
[66] Cartularium Abbathiae de Rievalle, Surtees Sy., vol. 83, pp. 354, 355.

"894. Feb. 26, 1534. Grant by Abbat Rowland to John Benson and Jenett, his wife, of a corrodie for term of their lives; grantees not to sell. The corrodie consists of — 'Everie week VI. gallons of the convent aill, and II. gallons of yoman aill, or els, as John Braithwat hath his aill, and II. gallons of grenhorn (last or weakest brew of malt), X. whit levery lowes and VI. rie lowes, and oons in a yere oon stone of tallowe, halfe a boschell of salt, and a boschell of oit meill; every day oon meisse of meitt (food), both fysche day and flesche day, ons of the day, served from the kitchyn, and to have a housse to dwell in, with a garthing, oon kow gaitt and oon lood of hay, oon lood of wood and oon of turwes to be assigned be a officer, at the cariage of the said John and Jenett.' If John die, his wife is only to have half, excepting the load of hay and cow-gate.

895. 26 March, 1526. Grant by Abbott William to John Braithwaitt and Alyson his wife, of a corrody for the term of their lives: not to sell the corrody on pain of forfeiture; the grantees living at Skiplom; corrody to consist of 'Everye weyke VI. gallons of convent haill, and II. gallons of the Abbottes hayll, IIII. gallons of grenhorne, X. lewe rye lowes and VI. rye lowes, oone bouschell of salte and halve a bouschell of hoyt meyll; and also for their lewery meyll oone beyffe to be delyvered to them at Martynmes by the assignment of the said Abbott or his officers; as it pleasse hym: and in the begynnyng of Lenten to have VII. salt Feych, LX. whyet heryn and LX. red heryn: and a clois bounding of Wedercoitt clois.' Also if they get tired of living at Skiplom, they shall give up their farm hold there and have a house to dwell in at the monastery, and a cow-gate, a load of hay carried to their door and also two loads of wood and two 'towrwes' carried to their door."

Corrodies varied widely in value. In a subsidy collected in the extended diocese of Lincoln in 1526, the names of all the corrodiers of each monastery are given with the value of their corrodies. These varied from 4s. 4d. to 13£ 6s. 8d. But the more usual values were 40s., 53s. 4d., 3£ 6s. 8d., 54s. 4d., and 5£ 6s. 8d.[67] There could naturally be no standard corrody. Local

---

[67] Subsidy Collected in the Diocese of Lincoln 1526, H. Salter, ed. Oxford 1909, cf. Valor Eccl. in Savine, Eng. Monasteries, etc., p. 243.

tradition, circumstances and influence contributed to produce the greatest diversity.

Admission to spiritual privileges (confraternity) very often accompanied a corrody.[68] The corrodier so privileged was made the participant in the intercessions and spiritual benefits of the monastery and after his death his name was remembered annually in the mass as if he were a deceased brother monk.[69] Occasionally we find that the corrodiers were expected to take some small part in the devotional routine of the community.[70]

Certain peculiarities or exceptional cases may here be briefly noted. Two men jointly could accept a corrody.[71] Three men each received corrodies in consideration for which they cancelled a bond of 40£ due them by the monastery.[72]

The corrody system may fairly be looked upon as part of the organized charity of the Middle Ages. Large sums were annually dispensed by the monasteries as alms. Part of this was in the form of corrodies. St. Albans provided thirteen corrodies for leprous women at St. Mary des Prez, in commemoration of the deceased Abbot William. Thirteen poor lepers were provided for at the Hospital of Ilford, Essex. Paupers were fed and cared for in many monasteries.[73] At the King's Hospital of Neuton, a commission was appointed to inquire into the sanity of a corrodier who was supposed to be deaf, but whose conduct created such an upheaval that the brethren thought he was mad.[74] According to the Valor Ecclesiasticus (1535) few monasteries had poor corrodiers and these were few in number. "Five at Lenton, Notts., six at Evesham, Worc., eleven at Athelney, Soms., twelve at Christ Church, Canterbury; thirteen both at Furness, Lanc. and Nostel, York.; eighteen at St. Peter's Westminster and twenty-four at Whalley, Lanc." At this late date "there can be no doubt that the number of poor living on

---

[68] Patent Rolls 1400, p. 368. Cartulary St. John Pontefract, Yorkshire Sy., vol. 25, II. p. 274.
[69] Letter Books Christ Church Canterbury, R. S., vol. 85, pt. 2, pp. 354, 456.
[70] Patent Rolls 1391, p. 484.
[71] Patent Rolls 1354, p. 136. 1399, p. 150.
[72] Patent Rolls 1375, p. 99.
[73] Chronica Monasterii S. Albani, R. S. vol. 28, pt. 5, p. 305. Dugdale vol. VII, p. 629, vol. VI, p. 479.
[74] Patent Rolls 1342, p. 648.

the liberality of a particular monastery was smaller, and probably much smaller than the number of the monks."[75]

Corrodies were also available as a form of old age pension. They likewise provided the means for compensating old and injured soldiers. Sometimes it was arranged that the corrodier should occupy some easy position in the economy of the monastery as long as he was able.[76] The Premonstratensians granted alms and weekly corrodies of two white loaves and two flasks of ale, to widows.[77] By means of the corrody the monastery provided a refuge for converts, probably Jews, and it also was found to be a convenient way to provide for the support of a university student.[78] The prior and convent of Bykenacre granted to John, son of Hugh de Swanesheth a corrody for life, including "shoe leather" and a suitable "robe of color" yearly and when John "shall go to the unversity (scolas) they shall pay him 10d. a week for his commons (ad connunem suam) and when he shall return from the university to dwell with them, they shall find him necessaries as above. John shall serve them and their successors humbly and faithfully without murmur or unbefitting contradiction, so long as he shall remain in secular habit or until he take the habit of religion."

The corrodies by purchase functioned in the society of the Middle Ages much like the annuities of our modern life insurance companies. In consideration of a fixed price paid by the corrodier the monastery undertook to maintain him for the balance of his life. The risk was carried by the monastery which had little reliable means of knowing how long the recipent was likely to live. Doubtless in many cases it was not a paying proposition for the monastery.

---

[75] Savine: English Monasteries, etc., p. 240, f.
[76] Calendar of Ancient Deeds, vol. II, B1857. Patent Rolls 1344, p. 374.
[77] Collectanea Anglo-premonstratensia III. Camden Sy. Series III, vol. 6, p. 215.
[78] Patent Rolls 1360, p. 364. Close Rolls 1287, p. 521 f.

CHAPTER V.   THE CORRODY AS A FORM OF PROPERTY

The corrody was a negotiable right. Hardly or only partly having the tangible qualities of a piece of leased property, it was a right to sustenance, and one in possession of this right frequently sold it to another. In 1343, Durand de Turade, clerk, sold to John de Alvyngton, a corrody which he enjoyed in the convent of Montecute. John had to swear that the would be good and faithful to the church and the prior and then the prior and convent issued to him letters patent granting to him a corrody for life. The king reviewed and confirmed the grant.[79] Such transactions probably took place frequently.[80] In the sixteenth century the practice of corrodiers selling corrodies must have been considered an abuse as grantees were often enjoined not to sell the corrody on pain of forfeiture.[81]

Corrodies that were purchased were often granted with the definite agreement that the corrody might be assigned to an attorney, even when it was provided that it should not be sold.[82] Again, this kind of corrody might be assigned to another during absence or it might be assigned to someone for one year after the death of the corrodier.[83]. There also appears to have been some tendency to make the corrody hereditable.[84] The son sometimes claimed and was granted the corrody of his father, but this was unusual and was confined to the second and fourth classes of recipients, i. e. the beneficiaries of royal and noble corrodies and the servants' corrody that was the equivalent of wages.[85]

Of course, the *claim to exact* a corrody was inherited with or

---

[79] Patent Rolls 1343, p. 132.
[80] Close Rolls 1349, p. 86, 1352 p. 467, 1371 p. 332.
[81] Cartularium Abbathiae de Rievalle, Surtees Sy. vol. 83, pp. 354 and 355.
[82] Letter Books Christ Church Canterbury, R. S. vol. 85, pt. 3, p. 13. Calendar Ancient Deeds, vol 1, B1498. Patent Rolls 1360, p. 440.
[83] Patent Rolls 1419, p. 180., 1420 p. 311.
[84] Registrum Malmesburiense, R. S. vol. 72, pt. 2, p. 298. Close Rolls 1350, p. 278.
[85] See pp. 10f, 19, 22.

without a will.[86] It was a customary right which one possessed on grounds of patronage or because of having been a founder or donor.[87] The right of a corrodier, the one who enjoyed the sustenance in a monastery, to transfer his sustenace to another is quite a different matter from the rights of those who claimed the privilege of exacting and disposing of a corrody.

At the close of the fourteenth century the custom of converting the corrody into a money payment, thereby making it practically a pension seems to have grown up in certain places. At St. Andwews, Tywardrayth, a corrody was given, of 2d. daily or 60s. 10d. yearly.[88] The fact that corrodies were so readily valued in marks and shillings would seem to indicate their commutation into money payments.[89]

The Roman law exerted considerable influence on the development of English common law, notably in the conception of property. The peculiar form of feudal tenure was supplanted by the idea of possession. This in English common law was developed into the doctrine of seisin, i. e. practical ownership was vested in him who had possession or who had the right to get possesion. So the adage ran, "Possession is nine-tenths of the law."

Under the system of writs, (i. e. the custom of notifying one to plead his case in the king's court, by a special writ of invitation of the king) the usual writ to be issued in order to prove possession in the courts, was that of novel disseisin. It is very significant that this writ was chosen by the lawyers of the thirteenth century, when a corrody was in arrears or had been denied. The plaintiff complained that he had been ejected, just as if the corrody had been a house or some piece of property. The corrody was much like a contract. It also resembled a piece of property. It was felt to be an "incorporeal thing." It was more real than an annuity, because it issued out of a certain place. It was less real than a rent because it was not

---

[86] See pp. 15, 16 and note 19.
[87] See pp. 14, 24 and note 55.
[88] Patent Rolls 1400, p. 281. Calendar of Ancient Deeds, vol. IV, A9353.
[89] Subsidy of Diocese of Lincoln 1526. Chronica Monasterii S. Albani, R. S. vol. 28, pt. 9, pp. 265, 268 and pt. 6, pp. 82, 181. Cf. in this connection Savine: English Monasteries on Eve of the Dissolution, p. 244 also the "Italian Relation" quoted above p. 23

charged on any specific land. In the assize of novel disseisin when a corrody was in question, the jurors were sent to view the monastery as a whole, whence the corrody was issued. In this way corrodies came to be considered as forms of real property.

By analogy and probably from the direct influence of the issuance of such writs for corrodies, this conception was extended to other incorporeal rights such as an annuity of hay and straw. In Richard II. reign an action for trespass was allowed for infringement of a beadle's customary right to claim certain gallons of beer. The assize of novel disseisin was provided by an act of 13 Edward I. Statute I. c. 25. "Forasmuch as there is no writ in the chancery whereby plaintiffs can have so speedy remedy as by a writ of novel disseisin", it was enacted that that writ should be issued for estovers of wood, corrodies, toll, passage, etc. Thus the actions about corrodies helped to develop and expand the application of the doctrine of seisin or possession, extending it to include all kinds of incorporeal rights. "A better example of medieval realism could hardly be given."[90]

Until 1285 the action for the recovery of a corrody took place in the ecclesiastical courts, after that date it was a temporal action, i. e. it could be brought in the king's court. It was originally and properly an ecclesiastical action, as Bracton (died 1268) pointed out, for the following reasons:[91] Because the corrody was issued by or proceeded from a religious house and therefore was a spiritual thing, recourse should be had not to the secular court but to the ecclesiastical. Further in granting corrodies, simony, the purchase of ecclesiastical offices might be committed,[92] of which the ecclesiastical courts properly took cognizance.

The grant of a corrody by purchase, was made a matter of court record, of which the Records of the Borough of Notting-

---

[90] Quoted from Pollock and Maitland, vol. II, p. 135, which work together with Holdsworth's History of English Law, vol. III, pp. 21, 86, 127, have provided the material for this summary.

[91] Bracton, de Legibus et Consuetudinibus, Bk. IV, c. xvi, sect. 7. (Rolls, vol. 70, pt. 3, pp. 147, 149.)

[92] See p. 37 f and note 117.

ham afford an interesting example. "To this court comes Brother John, Abbot of Neubo (Lincolnshire) and desires a writing to be enrolled under the tenor which follows: 'To all the faithful of Christ seeing or hearing this present writing, Brother John etc. and the Convent of that place, greeting in the Lord Everlasting. Know ye generally that we with the unanimous will and the consent of our whole chapter have given, granted and by this our present writing have confirmed to Sir Thomas Lambock of Nottingham, chaplain, the corrody of a canon every day for so long as he lives, to be fully received in our house of Neubo, comprising . . . The aforesaid Sir Thomas as a brother of our chapter is bound to keep and also conceal the secrets of the aforesaid House of Neubo, within and without doors, under the seal of confession and secrecy. In testimony etc!"[93] Other contracts were made in the king's court in the presence of the king's itinerant justices or at Westminster.[94] Then an inspeximus and confirmation of the charter was granted by the king.

Corrodies granted at the instance of the king, were given under the great seal of the abbey, upon the presentation of a writ de corrodio habendo. Samples of such writs may be found in the Appendix.

In the many actions brought in the king's court against the king, contesting his right to nominate to a corrody, the decision seems to be usually in favor of the abbot and convent. Doubtless many corrodies were imposed unjustly by the king, but where the abbot could afford to oppose the king and had the boldness and resource to do so, it was not difficult to show that the king had exceeded his rights. The plea of the monastery often began by denying that the writ had been served on the monastery. Then the charter of foundation was exhibited to prove that the king's progenitors had founded the abbey in free alms, frank almoigne, and that it had immunity, that is, freedom

---

[93] Records of the Borough of Nottingham, vol. I, p. 155 (1354). Cf. with regard to the "Secrets of the Abbey", Wilson, J. M., The Worcester Liber Albus, pp. 199f, where a rent collector for the priory of Worcester (1321) upon receiving a corrody swears "that he will reveal their secrets, or anything to their discredit, to no living creature."
[94] Chartulary of the Abbey of Ramsey, Rolls Series, vol. 79, pt. 2, p. 369. Yorkshire Archaeological Society, Record Series, vol. 13. Coucher Books of Selby, vol. II, pp. 330.

from all secular services, rents, etc. Sometimes appeal was made to the 'Articuli cleri' or the statute of 3 Edward I. or that of 1 Edward III. or to the king's own denial that the acceptance of a previous corrodier of his appointment, would prejudice the monastery as a precedent.[95] Sometimes the charter showed that, although of the king's advowson, the monastery was of another's foundation. They then proved that they held no lands or rents of the king that would warrant his demanding a corrody and that the previous admission of a corrodier was not of right but by way of courtesy.[96] Justice was done despite the king, but many monasteries submitted without a contest.

[95] Cartulary of the Abbey of Ramsey, Rolls Series, vol. 79, pt. 3, pp. 99–108. Registrum Prioratus Beatae Mariae Wigorniensis, Camden Sy., vol. 91, pp. 175–180, cxxv.
[96] Patent Rolls, 1340 p. 67 f. 1341 p. 293 f. 1346 p. 83 f.

CHAPTER VI. ABUSES OF THE SYSTEM AND EFFORTS AT REFORM

A survey of the sources indicates that the system of granting corrodies was often a form of graft, both royal and ecclesiastical. As the worldly interests of the monasteries increased it seemed wise for them to have a friend in the person of the king, and the latter took advantage of the opportunity to impose on the monks. His promise "to promote the affairs of the monastery thereafter" did not give much comfort. The king continually promised that a grant of a corrody to his appointee would not prejudice the monastery by way of precedent, yet he continued to send his appointees who usually forced their claims on the liberality of the convent.[97] In 1336 Edward III. gave to Christ Church, Canterbury, a release from the obligation of granting any pensions or corrodies in the future, but within three years the convent resisted the request of a corrody for Nicholas Wycombe, the king's watchman. Notwithstanding, it appears that Nicholas received the corrody,[98] and others after him, for Richard II., in 1395, was petitioned to renew the release and did so on consideration that the convent annually on the festivals of the Passion and Translation of St. Edmund, King and Martyr, remember in the mass the late Queen Anna and the King himself after his decease.[99]

In many cases where a monastery admitted a corrodier at the request of the king, his highness acknowledged that it was not because the house was of royal foundation or because it held any land in chief from the king. He allowed that it was not required to grant a corrody, although such grants had been made before and he assured them that this grant, springing from the convent's free and voluntary desire, would not in the future prejudice their house as a precedent. This did not prevent him

---

[97] Cf. Letter Books of the Monastery of Christ Church Canterbury, Rolls Series, vol. 85, pt. 1, p. 42, with pt. 2, p. 235.
[98] Cf. in the above pt. 2, pp. 122, 212, 234, with pt. 3, p. 35.
[99] Letter Books of the Monastery of Christ Church Canterbury, Rolls Series, vol. 85, pt. 3, pp. 32–41.

however, from demanding another corrody of the same house within a year or two.[100] Again, such royal letters patent were sometimes granted without the knowledge and consent of the king[101] and when they were, they were not always respected. Alice Fitz Rauf, armed with such royal writ for St. John's Hospital, Oxford, was assaulted at night, her face veiled and she was thrown into a filthy place in the streets of Oxford. When she revived, the royal writ was gone. Among those accused of this rude and violent deed, we find the name of the Master of the Hospital.[102]

That many monasteries granted corrodies in order to curry favor with the king or out of fear, is reflected in official documents.[103] Despite the fact that Edward III. had dispensed Stoneleye from granting a corrody, they bestowed one at the request of Henry IV. "because they dared not resist his will."

The custom of appointing to a corrody before it became vacant was common.[104] Edward III. had a particularly bad memory in this respect. He would promise a corrody during the life of its incumbent and then when it was vacated he would grant it to another. Afterwards he would usually remember that he had granted the corrody "a long time before" and wholly revoke the letters patent that he had lately issued. This aroused a contest and someone was the loser. This device was frequently resorted to but we have no intimation for what considerations the letters patent were granted.[105] In one instance at least it may have been out of simple gratitude, to his royal father's baker, for the cakes and cookies that Edward III. enjoyed in his boyhood. In 1356, Edward III. issued a pardon to Adam and Walter atte More for having obtained from the Abbey of Middleton the guest house with grounds, certain rents and two livings and for entering into possession of the same without his license.

---

[100] Calendar of Patent Rolls, 1353, p. 479, (Fountains); 1342, p. 491; and 1343, p. 135, (St. Benet, Hulme).
[101] Calendar of Patent Rolls, 1341, pp. 168, 178.
[102] Calendar of Patent Rolls, 1341, pp. 214, 215, 217, 311.
[103] Calendar of Close Rolls, 1293, p. 279. Calendar of Patent Rolls, 1399, p. 176.
[104] Calendar of Patent Rolls, 1344, p. 374 and 1346, p. 80.
[105] Calendar of Patent Rolls, 1341, pp. 168, 178. 1342, pp. 496, 517, 564. 1343, p. 14. 1357, p. 601. 1495, p. 13.

With his pardon he granted license to retain what they had illegally secured.[106]

In order to be free from such royal imposition many monasteries bribed the king by a grant of land or a gift of money.[107] He even accepted money "as a subvention toward his expenses", for giving monasteries the assurance that the grants of corrodies in the past and present would not prejudice the abbey as a precedent.[108] The monastery had to pay one way or the other unless it was in a position to resist the king's will and bring the case into court. Even then when the decision was rendered for the monastery, they sometimes paid for the royal favor, as in the case last cited.

Often the appointees of the king had several incomes granted them as in the case of Master John Somerseth[109] who for teaching Henry VI. and preserving his health, received a grant of 60£ per year from the king, 40£ per year at the hands of the Sheriff of London and a corrody at Cirencester. In the thirteenth century, we have two instances recorded of corrodies being unjustly extorted from St. Alban's.[110] In the first case, Childewicke, a brother-in-law of John Mansel, advisor to the king, resorts to spurious charters to gain his end. In the second instance, Earl Edmund, son of Henry III. forced the Abbey to grant a corrody to one of his family.

A corrody might be demanded of a monastery and attached to some petty local position such as fosgraveship or the care of the water of Fosse at St. Mary's, York.[111] That others than the king found the monasteries a great convenience in this way is illustrated in the case of John Middleton and his son Thomas who each by separate grants released all rights in their lands at Esthamme and Westhamme to William de Monte Revelli, who in turn granted to each severally and to their wives a mainte-

---

[106] Calendar of Patent Rolls, 1356, p. 475.
[107] Chronica Monasterii S. Albanii, Rolls Series, vol. 28, pt. 7, p. 113. Calendar of Ancient Deeds, vol. III., A5461. Calendar of Patent Rolls, 1482, p. 307.
[108] Calendar of Patent Rolls, 1347, p. 539.
[109] Calendar of Patent Rolls, 1432, p. 241.
[110] Chronica Monasterii S. Albani, Rolls Series, vol. 28, pt. 5, p. 318 and pt. 7, pp. 100 and 394.
[111] Calendar of Patent Rolls, 1495, p. 13.

nance for life of 4d daily and two robes and 20s. yearly, *until they be provided with a suitable corrody in a religious house.* If they should come into the service of William the latter is acquitted of the maintenance or corrody. If they later leave his service they have the right to the maintenance or the corrody. If William transgress in this, John or Thomas may destrain all his goods in England and Gascony.[112] Under such an arrangement, whenever William dismissed John or Thomas from his service he had to find him a living in some monastery or else pay the equivalent out of his own pocket. He must have been in a position to make such demands upon one or more religious houses and very likely did.

The Abbots very often favored their relatives and friends. At Shrewsbury, the Abbot of St. Peter and St. Paul granted to his sister and her husband John Copland very extensive corrodies that included the tithes of sheaves and hay of two towns of the Abbey, the house which they occupied in the town, the husband's shop, a messuage, a meadow and twelve cartloads of wood annually.[113] This must have made the abbot's brother-in-law one of the most prosperous business men in the town. At St. Albans, Abbot Roger (1290) "whom no one wished or dared to resist" burdened the Abbey with liveries sold to his friends. A corrody granted in this fashion for the manor of Pinesfield amounted to the annual value of 30£.[114]

The Abbots naturally exerted considerable influence in the policy to be adopted toward corrodies from time to time. Normally the corrody could be granted only by the Abbot with the consent of the whole convent but cases of usurpation of authority by the Abbot are frequent. The famous Abbot Sampson of Bury St. Edmunds (1199) had his way despite the chapter, regarding the corrody of the gate-keeper. At the Abbey of Ramsey the prohibition against granting corrodies without the common consent was reiterated within one decade. In a single year (1221) we find two papal prohibitions, forbidding the Abbots

---

[112] Calendar of Close Rolls, 1279, p. 562.
[113] Calendar of Ancient Deeds, vol. V, 11470.
[114] Chronica Monasterii S. Albani, Rolls Series, vol. 28, pt. 5, p. 484.

of Persore and Winchelcumb to grant corrodies without the consent of the convent.[115]

The monks also were not above extortionate practices. At Scarboro (1139?) Simon Gamel granted to the monastery of St. John Pontefract certain rents in the town in return for a corrody. Later when he fell into "great necessity" he quitclaimed the corrody for half a mark of silver promising that the monks were not to be disturbed in the collection of the rents which had been in his former gift. Thus instead of his rents he now had a half mark of silver, which doubtless was soon spent.[116]

At the same monastery in 1236, Germanus, a clerk, the son of Adam, chaplain of Ledstone, surrendered all his estate to the monastery in consideration of a corrody, such as a gate-keeper received and in addition 5s. yearly for life. By a charter granted by *him*[117] he promised to abide by this corrody and to celebrate the mass for the dead to which the monks of Pontefract were bound. This Germanus was promoted to the priesthood by the monastery so that probably we have here an instance showing how a small corrody could be used to cover up a case of simony. The fact that the charter was granted by the ordinand and was his promise to remain satisfied with the small corrody looks rather suspicious.

Simony, unscrupulous extortion, favoritism, illegal and highhanded action, all followed in the wake of the corrody system. An intimate acquaintance with the sources relative to corrodies opens up a questionable side in the moral life, public and private, secular and religious, of the Middle Ages. They illustrate how thoroughly secularized the Church of the Middle Ages was; how it was borne down by the weight of its own machinery.

Popes, bishops, kings and nobility each in his own way did what he could to restrict the granting of corrodies. Papal pro-

---

[115] Memorials of St. Edmund's Abbey, Rolls Series, vol. 96, pt. 1, p. 315, f. Cartulary of the Abbey of Ramsey, vol. 79, pt. 2, pp. 198, 213. Calendar of Papal Registers, vol. I, pp. 78, 80.

[116] Cartulary of St. John Pontefract, vol. II, Yorkshire Archæological Sy., vol. 30, p. 523.

[117] Cartulary of St. John of Pontefract, vol. I, Yorkshire Archaeological Sy., vol. 25, p. 223.

hibibtions against the granting of any corrodies whatever (except to monks and those personally engaged in the service of the monastery) were issued to St. Augustine's Canterbury in 1256 and to Norwich in 1400. Two years afterwards at the latter place the sale of corrodies led to a conflict with the Bishop of Norwich and the Pope issued a charter confirming the Archbishop of Canterbury as an arbitrator. On the other hand, when the Rector of the Augustinian hospital of Southwerk granted corrodies contrary to his oath given to the Bishop of Winchester he was absolved and rehabilitated.[118]

In 1455, the Pope issued a mandate to the prior and convent of the Augustinian monastery of St. Mary Brunton, diocese of Bath and Wells, as follows: — "The Pope has learned that in England there has prevailed a custom or rather abuse, according to which immovable goods and fees and rights, belonging to monasteries and other regular places and many other ecclesiastical rents called corrodies have for a money consideration been granted for life under letters, even bearing the conventual seals, to nobles and other laymen, to farm or under a yearly cess, to the great hurt of the said monasteries and places, some of which nobles, etc., are said to have obtained and to be daily obtaining letters of confirmation. Seeing that, as the Pope has learned, their monastery is burdened in such ways to the sum of 40£ sterling a year, he orders them under pain of excommunication to abstain in future from such grants and alienation of fees, corrodies, etc., and the said nobles under like pain to abstain and to induce others to abstain from seeking, buying, receiving corrodies, etc., and further orders, the prior and convent to procure under the same penalty the revocation of such as have been alienated, letters notwithstanding."[119]

This recently published document tells us many interesting facts. The practice of granting and selling corrodies to laymen was an essentially English custom. It was looked upon by churchmen as an abuse and one that had become a serious economic drain. The corrody was considered to be a form of rent, granted under the great seal of the convent to all kinds of laity,

---
[118] Calendar of Papal Registers, vol. I, p. 335, vol IV, p. 273 and pp. 586, 497.
[119] Calendar of Papal Letters, vol. XI, p. 96.

great and small, who to make their rights sure, obtained letters of confirmation from the king. The custom had grown to such alarming proportions that it claimed the attention of the Papacy.

Bishops also had the immediate right of supervising the granting of corrodies. In the foundation charter of the priory of Maxstoke, granted (1339) by William Clinton, Count of Huntingdon, the creation of any corrody or pension was forbidden except for "evident utility or inevitable necessity of which the bishop of the place at the time shall be the judge and shall first give his approval."[120] In the arch-episcopal visitation, among the questions regularly asked of the monasteries were these:— "Whether there were any corrodies or pensions, why and what had been granted, and if so, to whom and by whom, and for what time and by what authority."[121] All the bishops from Durham to Exeter were aroused to the necessity of checking and controlling this abuse.[122] Between 1422 and 1435, twenty episcopal injunctions in the Diocese of Lincoln alone have come down to us, prohibiting the granting of corrodies except with episcopal license.[123] The injunctions are modelled upon a common formula which runs as follows:— "Furthermore, we enjoin upon you the prior under pain of your deprivation and final removal from your office and dignity, that henceforward you sell or grant to no persons whatsoever corrodies, pensions, annuities or liveries for a fixed time, term of life or in perpetuity, unless you have first asked and obtained license of us or our successors for a lawful and needful cause set forth to us or to the same our successors and approved by us or them, with the accession thereunto of the express consent and assent of the whole convent or of the greater and sounder part of the same."[124]

---

[120] Dugdale, vol. VI, p. 525.
[121] Coucher Books of Selby, vol. II, Yorkshire Archaeological Sy., Record Series, vol. 13, p. 368.
[122] Registrum Palatimum Dunelmense, Rolls Series, vol. 62, pt. 4, p. 390 and pt. 2, pp. 727 ff. Oliver: Monasticon, p. 18, (III.) Cant. & York Sy., vol. 7 (1911), p. 54 f. Cartularium Prioratus de Gyseburne, Surtees Sy., vol. 89, (1891) pp. 378, 398, 401.
[123] Visitations of Religious Houses in Diocese of Lincoln, vol. II, Cant. & York Sy., vol. 17, (1915) pp. 4, 10, 19, 24, 28, 31, 39, 43, 47, 49, 56, 77, 80, 87, 96, 99, 101, 111, 121, 127.
[124] Visitattions of Religious Houses in Diocese of Lincoln, vol. II, Cant. & York Sy., vol. 17 (1915), p. 111.

Within the monastic organization where a monastery had a cell or daughter monastery, the consent of the Abbot of the mother house was necessary before a corrody could be granted by the cell. The master and brethren of the Hospital of St. John Baptist, Coventry, were not to presume to sell or grant a corrody without the license of the Prior of Coventry. The prior of Belvoir took an oath to the Abbot of St. Alban's not to sell a corrody without his license.[125]

Noble patrons also, endeavored to restrict the granting of corrodies. Richard, Earl of Arundel, claiming the patronage of St. Mary's, Castleacre, in the diocese of Norwich, exacted from the prior an oath not to alienate woods, corrodies or other possessions without his consent.[126]

The king, although he was himself the greatest offender in demanding the grant of corrodies, was foremost in the effort to check the granting of them. He seems to have claimed the right of confirming all grants, for which confirmation there was a charge, usually of one-half mark.[127] The Charter Rolls contain many charters of quittance of corrodies.[128] When on account of the war with France, the king appointed guardians for a monastery, they were directed to seize all corrodies and to eject the holders. This was done in many instances when the monastery was in a bad financial state. Administrators were appointed who usually relieved the house of these charges.[129]

The thirteenth and fourteenth centuries saw a great development of law by legislation. The condition of the monasteries and the pleas of the clergy combined to put laws against the abuse of corrodies on the statute books. The First Statute of Westminster, 3 Edward I. (1275) has been quoted above. The abuse not being abated, 2 Edward II. (1309) renews the previous statute and quotes it. A few years later (1316) the so-called Articuli Cleri, the responses which King Edward II. made at York to the urgent demands of the clergy refer to the Statute

---

[125] Dugdale, vol. VII, p. 660, vol. III, p. 291.
[126] Calendar of Papal Registers, vol. V, p. 78 (1405).
[127] Calendar of Patent Rolls, 1356, p. 475.
[128] Calendar of Charter Rolls, vol. V. pp. 162 (1359), 214 (1368), 227 (1372), 433 (1407), 446 (1412) although of patronage of the king, p. 456 (1413), 470 (1414).
[129] Calendar of Patent Rolls, 1357, p. 523, p. 74 f. 1366 p. 225, 1366 p. 244, 1435 p. 473.

of Edward I. and expand its application.[130] To the request that the "king and the great men of the realm do not charge religious houses, or spiritual persons, for corrodies, pensions or provisions in the religious houses," the king determined that "henceforth they shall not be unduly charged." "If the contrary be done, by great men and others," remedy is to be found in the statutes of Edward I. and "like remedy shall be made for corrodies and pensions extracted by compulsion whereof no mention is made in the statutes." I take this to mean that the statute of Westminster did not specify compulsion so it is here especially included as a ground for legal action. In the Statute of Marlborough, 1 Edward III. (1326) upon the earnest solicitation of the bishops and abbots of the realm, the king himself promises to exact no more corrodies, "that from henceforth he will no more such things desire, but where he ought." Judging from his frequent demands during the balance of his long reign, the king thought his rights in the matter were very extensive. In statutes of 1340, 1344, and 1377, the purveyance of the goods of spiritual persons and houses is forbidden, but corrodies are not specifically mentioned, the previous statutes being both sufficient and also futile.[131] The custom went on sapping the resources and wearing down the discipline of the monasteries, to the very end. With the disappearance of the monasteries went the destruction of the corrody system.

---

[130] Statutes of the Realm, vol. I, p. 171, also in Gee and Hardy; Documents, etc., pp. 96 ff.
[131] Statutes of the Realm, vol. I. —
   3 Ed. I. (1275) p. 26.
   2 Ed. II. (1309) p. 153.
   9 Ed. II. (1316) p. 171.
   1 Ed. III. (1326) p. 255, f. Statute 2, c. 10.
  14 Ed. III. (1340) p. 293. Statute 4, c. 1.
  18 Ed. III. (1344) p. 303. Statute 3, c. 4.
   1 Rich. II. (1377) Vol. II, p. 1, c. 3.

CHAPTER VII. CORRODIES AS A FACTOR IN MONASTIC DECLINE

The influence of the corrody system upon monastic life and institutions must have been considerable. It opened the doors of the monastery to the introduction of four quite distinct groups of lay people, none of whom took vows, or entered into the life and spirit of the monastic routine or participated in any way except to enjoy the comfort and retirement which a great religious house could provide. These groups were:— 1) the ever increasing number of servants and agents of the monastery who conducted its worldly business, 2) the sick, the poor and the weak-minded who were the beneficiaries of the monastic charity; 3) a very large number of 'corrodiers by purchase,' mostly old couples, unmarried women, widowers, etc., who lacking a home were financially able to obtain one by the purchase of a corrody that often provided comforts and privileges wholly denied to the monastic brethren themselves, and 4) people, frequently of the better class who through the favor of the king or some influential noble, received in the monastery a very comfortable living for the balance of their lives. Sometimes quite young people were the holders of corrodies.[132]

It was inevitable that the presence of such a large number of unprofessed in the monastery, a number usually exceeding the number of monks or nuns, was detrimental to monastic discipline, and the monastic ideal. The character of these outsiders might be more than questionable, so that it sometimes was stipulated that the corrodier do not introduce bad or forbidden women for immoral purposes, "which if he shall do and it be proved against him, he shall pay 20s. within one month or lose his corrody for one whole year."[133] Even the most innocent diversions of the corrodiers operated in time to undermine the monastic ideal. For example, a small group of congenial friends around the chess-board would be quite sufficient to wear down

---
[132] Dugdale, vol. II, p. 238. (St. Albans 1146).
[133] Calendar of Patent Rolls, 1400, p. 281.

and disrupt the discipline of the religious life. Corrodiers frequently received extra portions of food on fast days.[134]

In quite another way the corrody had a great influence upon monastic institutions, namely in the acquisition of property. The possession of vast landed estates, sometimes scattered in different parts of England, or often stretching in contiguous tracts for twenty or thirty miles, converted the monastic house into a big business corporation. The corrody was a popular and ready means to increase its landed property.[135] At times a small annual payment was made to the donor and heirs. Instead of a piece of land, it was occasionally the rental of a mill for which the corrody was granted.[136]

The case of the Hospital of St. Katherine's by the Tower of London shows how zeal in this matter grew apace. In 1374 in consideration for tenements, shops and houses located in the parish of St. Mary, Abbey Church, an extensive corrody was granted that included land within the hospital and the right to build thereon. In the following year, 1375, a corrody was granted to another person for a "certain sum", with land and the right to build on it. The corrodiers after having built their house could live there with their servants or they could sublet, during their lives, if they chose, but they could not sell without special license. In the following year, 1376, more land for building was similarly granted and in 1377 a woman received a corrody with the use of a house in the Hospital on the condition that at her own charge, she build at the Hospital's manor of Reynham in Kent a water mill within one year, to be maintained by the warden, brethren and sisters of the Hospital.[137] This institution was evidently over-zealous in business matters, but the ideal of poverty was not promoted by such an active interest in this world's goods. The ambitious schemes of abbots to enlarge the buildings of the convent or to erect a large and im-

---

[134] Wilson, J. M., Worcester Liber Albus, pp. 85 f.
[135] Cartulary of the Abbey of Ramsey, Rolls Series, vol. 79, pt. 2, p. 369. Coucher Books of Selby, Yorkshire Archaeological Sy., vol. 13, p. 330. Calendar of Ancient Deeds, vol. II, A 1888 and vol. III, A 4226.
[136] Cartulary of St. John of Pontefract, vol. I, Yorkshire Archaeological Sy., vol. 25, p. 191 and p. 274 and p. 223. Cartulary of St. John of Pontefract, vol. II. York. Arch. Sy., vol. 30, p. 573.
[137] Calendar of Patent Rolls, 1874, p. 450. 1375, p. 133. 1376, p. 345. 1377, p. 483 f.

pressive church, required ready money and very largely promoted the sale of corrodies.[138] The corrody contributed largely to that accumulation of wealth which led directly to monastic decline and subjected the monasteries to criticism in both state and church.

That the granting of corrodies was felt to be disadvantageous and detrimental to the healthy development of religious life is shown in the charters founding the King's chapels at Westminster and Windsor (1353, 1354). Both king and clergy agreed that when starting these new royal foundations, no pension, corrody or maintenance of any sort should be granted at the request of the king or his successors.[139]

The Abbey of St. Albans (1324) presents us with a fair illustration of how the monasteries were struggling under a financial burden and endeavoring to escape it through bad financing.[140] For years an annual pension of ten marks derived from the manor of Hartburn in the diocese of Durham, had been paid to Sir Hugh of Bolebeke, his heirs, etc., or to one cleric appointed by him. Due to the constant wars between the English and the Scotch, the manor of Hartburn became impoverished, so the Abbot and convent redeemed the pension by paying £20 to Sir John of Lancaster, Lord of Bolabeke, who renounced all claim to the pensions. This new burden of £20 fell upon Sir John Redburn, the Refectorer, who was administering the finances. In order to raise the money he sold two corrodies to a woman and her son. In such ways the monasteries were continually redeeming old corrodies by granting new ones, thus merely shifting instead of relieving the burden.

Corrodies, often granted to young people and sometimes made hereditable, might add to the landed possessions of a house; but its future was thereby mortgaged, its worldly cares increased and the business machinery of the Abbey made more complicated. Abbot Hugh of St. Alban's, who died in 1326, left the monastery 5000 marks in debt. He had been especially

---

[138] Oliver; Monasticon p. 18 (III). Chronica Monasterii S. Albani, Rolls Series, vol. 28, pt. 4, p. 454.
[139] Calendar of Charter Rolls, vol. V, pp. 129 and 136.
[140] Chronica Monasterii S. Albani, Rolls Series, vol. 28, pt. 6, p. 118.

depressed by corrodies that had been sold in the time of three of his predecessors at the end of the previous century. The corrodies then being enjoyed amounted to an annual sum of £299 and the pensions to £83. The corrodiers were more than fifty-four in number.

The monks endeavored to escape all kinds of debts and obligations by the granting of corrodies.[141] The Master of St. Leonard's Hospital, York, having raised all the money he could and having redeemed two corrodies of long standing, was unable to pay the wool demanded for the king, so he received license to sell two more corrodies. The ready money obtained in this way met an urgent need but was soon gone. The corrody, however, continued for years as a drain on the wealth of the monastery. The statement by Alexander Savine, in his valuable study, "The English Monasteries on the Eve of the Dissolution", that "these people", referring to the corrodiers by purchase, "were of no expense at all to the house", is not justified by the evidence.[142] In the Calendar of Papal Registers, in entries under 1397 and 1401, two monasteries were in financial distress, due partly at least, to the accumulation of corrodies.[143] In 1366 a commission was appointed by Edward III. to abolish the corrodies at La Bremere, County Oxford, "so miserably depressed and burdened by corrodies granted to suspected persons of foul character that the divine worship has ceased and alms and other pious works are withdrawn and there is danger of the dispersal of the monks there through lack of sustenance". The persons may not have been of such foul character as the king made them out to be and Edward III. was himself a great offender in the imposition of corrodies, but the fact remains that the monastery was in a bad way financially and this was attributed to the corrodies. A few years later the king ordered the Bishop of Worcester to make a visitation of St. Augustine's, Bristol, and to reduce the number of corrodies there, the abbey having been brought low by the sale and grant of the same.[144]

---
[141] Calendar of Close Rolls, 1365, p. 204; Calendar of Patent Rolls, 1375, p. 99; Calendar of Patent Rolls, 1347, p. 366.
[142] Oxford Studies in Social and Legal History, vol I, p. 244.
[143] Calendar of Papal Registers, vol. IV, 1397, p. 15. 1401, p. 347.
[144] Patent Rolls 1366, p. 244. Close Rolls 1371, p. 259.

At Melsa in 1396 upon the death of Abbot William there were fifteen corrodies amounting in value to £61 9s. 7d. although he had redeemed corrodies granted by his predecessors to the annual value of £10 6s. 8d. As it has been pointd out, Abbot William of Dringhow raised by the sale of corrodies £500, or what was equivalent to five-sixths of one year's income.[145] If fifteen corrodies amounted in value to over £60, £500 must have represented over a hundred corrodies, assuming for the sake of argument, that they averaged about the same value. Many of these became extinct through death or redemption and the number of corrodies in a given monastery fluctuated greatly even in a single generation.

Thus in three ways the granting of corrodies promoted the decline of monastic life in England. The presence of numbers of corrodiers in the convent broke down discipline and the monastic ideal. The corrody was used to increase the landed estates of the monastery and thereby added to the burden and complexity of administration as well as to the wealth and luxury of the houses. Finally the corrodies, unless granted for land, were not paying investments. New corrodies had to be sold in order to buy up and relieve the monastery of the burden of the old ones.

Corrodies continued to be granted up to the dissolution of the lesser monasteries, 1536 and after.[146] In the act by which the lesser monasteries were suppressed it was provided that the king might by letters patent, grant the lands and other property of the monasteries, except that the corrodies and other rents were to be continued to the holders of them as if the monastery had not been suppressed. Those to whom the monastic property had been granted took over all obligations, including the corrodies, and maintained them. But in some monasteries, when they saw that the dissolution was imminent, the abbots granted new corrodies and in other ways disposed of the wealth of the house. These corrodies were declared void by the statutes if granted within one year previous to the dissolution, unless they were the renewal of old and customary charges. All rents and annuities

---

[145] Chronica Monasterii de Melsa, R. S. vol. 43, pt. 3, pp. 227 and XIII, LXVII.
[146] Oliver: Monasticon, pp. 92, 340.

of heirs and donors were to be kept intact for them as if the monasteries had not been suppressed. The same conditions were imposed in the act dissolving the greater monasteries (1539) and, under Edward VI., in the act dissolving the chantries (1547.) [147]

How were these conditions observed? In many cases Henry VIII. granted the monastic lands with a covenant of discharge against pensions, corrodies, etc., which released the recipients of monastic estates from maintaining the corrodies. In this case, suit could be brought only in the Court of Augmentations which had been recently set up for this purpose. All corrodies were recoverable by the holders at law if they had been paid within ten years prior to the act of 35 Henry VIII. (1543).[148] In many cases, the Court of Augmentations substituted a cash annuity or pension for the corrody. To be specific, in 1533 at Ford Abbey, in the diocese of Exeter, a corrody consisting of a house and garden, food and fuel, was granted to William Mitchell and his wife Alice or their assigns, with an annuity of eight marks. In the Augmentations Court, the lease was allowed to stand. A corrody granted to Ralph Bagshowe and wife for a consideration of £20 was allowed as a valid agreement in the Court of Augmentations, but only the pension of eight marks yearly was confirmed. As late as 1537, a corrody in the same Abbey was granted to William Tyler, M. A., consisting of an annuity of £3 6s. 8d. with room and daily meals and an annual gown, all as a compensation for teaching grammar. In 1540 the Court of Augmentations allowed Tyler 60s. annually.[149] At Tavistock and Tywardreth, corrodiers had their holdings commuted into annuities of £6, £5 and £3 6s. 8d.[150]

We may conclude from these cases that the corrodies were generally commuted into yearly pensions and were continued to their holders by the new owners of the property, until death removed the corrodiers. The institution then became extinct, a relic of the days gone by.

---
[147] Statutes of the Realm, vol. III, p. 575. 27 Henry VIII, c. 28.
         vol. III, p. 733. 31 Henry VIII, c. 13.
         vol. IV, p. 24. 1 Edward VI, c. 14.
[148] Statutes of the Realm, vol. III, p. 918. 35 Henry VIII, c. 19.
[149] Oliver; Monasticon, p. 340.
[150] Oliver; Monasticon, pp. 47, 92.

APPENDIX I

COGNATES OF CON-REDUM

Icel.	reiði	tackle, harness.
	reiðt	raid.
	greiði	account, service, arrangement.
	greiðr	ready.
	greiða	to equip.
Old Eng.	geræde	ready.
Eng.	ready.	
	road and ride (questionable)	
Ger.	bereiten (ge-reiten)	to prepare.
	bereits	ready, prepared.
Mid. Low Ger.	gerēde	equipment.
Old High Ger.	reita	raid.
	reiti	ready.
	reidan	to ride.
Mid. High Ger.	gereide	harness, utensils.
Swedish	reda	order, to set in order.
Old Irish	riadaim	to go.
Gothic	raidjan	to determine, arrange.
	geraidjan	to get ready.
	*garaidjo	(Hypothetical form).

DERIVITIVES OF CON-REDUM

Old Fr.	conrei, later conroi	preparation.
		1. troop or company.
		2. refreshment, law of the gite.
		3. law of those who convey merchandise.
	conreer	to prepare, hence curry leather.
Provencal	conre, conrei	equipage, provision.
	correar	to equip.
Old Sp.	conreo	provision or care in preservation of a thing.
Sp.	correo	provisions for letters, post.
Port.	correia	provisions for letters, post.
It.	corredo	outfit, equipage.
	corredare	to fit out.

Eng.	curry	from old Fr. conreer.
	array	from Romanic type ad-redare.
	conrey	outfit, company of troops, provision.
	(obsolete)	

NOTE — See the postage stamps of Spain, Portugal and nearly all South American countries for the use of the word correo and correia, meaning post.

APPENDIX II

SAMPLES OF THE WRIT DE CORRODIO HABENDO FROM REGISTER OF WRITS 1634 (p. 264.)

Rex, dilectissimis sibi in Christo priori & conventui de H. salutem. Volentes dilecto Valecto nostro S. de sustentatione congrua providere: ipsum ad vos duximus transmittendum rogantes quatenus ipsum S. in domum vestram prædictam admittentes, ei talem sustentationem in omnibus, qualem P. iam defunctus habuit dum vixit in eadem, ministrari, & ei literas vestras communi sigillo domus vestae signatas, mentionem de his quae de eadem domo vestra sic percipiet facientes, sibi super hoc fieri, & ei liberari faciatis, pro quo vobis in agendis domus vestrae praedictae teneri volumus specialius in futuro. Et quid inde ad hunc rogatum nostrum duxeritis faciendum: nobis rescribatis per praesentium portatorem. T. &c.

Statute 1st Edward III. c. XI.

Rex etc. Volentes de gratia nostra speciali dilectae nobis G. nuper unae domicellarum amitae nostrae nuper comitissae de M. quae ultimo obiit, cui de sustentatione sua per nos nondum est provisum, de hujusmodi sustentatione providere, ipsam ad vos duximus destinandam, mandantes sicut alias mandavimus, quatenus eandem Gertrudem in domum vestram praedictam admittentes, & talem sustentationem ut in victu et vestitu et aliis necessariis, qualem Margareta iam. defuncta, etc.

Rex, vic' N. salutem. Si I de A. fecerit &c. tunc pone &c. I. abbatem de C. quod fit &c. ostensurus quare cum nos nuper volentes eidem I. praetextu boni seruitis sui tam domino E. nuper regi Angl' patri nostro quam nobis impensi de sustentatione congrua providere, ipsum ad praefatum abbatem et ejusdem loci conventum duxerimus transmittendum, mandantes quatenus ipsum I. in domum suam praedictam admitterent, et ei talem sustentationem in omnibus quoad vixerit de eadem domo percipiend', qualem Richardus defunctus dum vixit in domo sua praedicta ad rogatum dicti patris nostri in eadum habuit, ministrari, eique literas suas patentes de praedicta sustentatione sigillo communi domus suae praedictae signatas fieri facerent, vel causam nobis significarent quare mandatis nostris alias eis inde directis minime paruerunt, vel quod idem abbas esset coram nobis a die sancti Hillarii &c. proximo praeterito ubicumque tunc essemus in Anglia, ostensurus quare mandatis nostris praedictis toties ei inde directis parere contempsit et breve nostrum ei inde directum haberet tunc ibidem; idem abbas spretis mandatis nostris praedictis ut accepimus, praefatum Iohannem in domum suam praedictam admittere, & ei talem sustentationem quoad vixerit de domo sua .praedicta percipiendam, qualem praedictus Richardus dum vixit ad rogatum dicti patris nostri de eadem domo percepit, ministrare, & literas suas patentes sigillo communi domus suae signatas ei inde facere, vel causam, quare praemissa facere noluit vel non potuit, nobis significare, vel coram nobis ad diem praedictum venire, aut breve nostrum ei inde directum ibidem retornare non curavit, in nostri ad mandatorum nostrorum praedictorum contemptum manifestum, & grave damnum ipsius Iohannis ut dicit. Et habeas ibi hoc breve. T. &c.

APPENDIX III

REFERENCES

Calendar of Ancient Deeds.
Calendar of Charter Rolls.
Calendar of Close Rolls.
Calendar of Documents Preserved in France.
Calendar of Papal Registers.   Papal Letters.
Calendar of Patent Rolls.
Camden Society Publications.
    Vol. 37. Relation of the Island of England. ed. C. A. Sneyd, 1847.

Vol. 60. Grants, etc., from the Crown during the Reign of Edward V. ed. J. G. Nichols, 1854.
Vol. 65. Knights Hospitallers in England. ed. L. B. Larking and J. M. Kemble, 1857.
Vol. 69. Domesday of St. Paul's. 1222. ed. W. H. Hale, 1858.
Vol. 91. Registrum Prioratus Beatae Mariae Wigorniensis, ed. W. H. Hale, 1865.
New Series. Vol. 51 Accounts of Obedientiaries of Abingdon Abbey. ed. R. E. G. Kirk, 1892.
Third Series. Vol. 12. Collectanea Anglo-Premonstratensia. ed. F. A. Gasquet. Vol. III. 1906.
Canterbury and York Society.
Vol. 7. Registrum Episcoporum Londoniensium, 1304-1338. ed. R. C. Fowler, 1911.
Vol. 17. Visitations of Religious Houses in Diocese of Lincoln, Vol. II. ed. A. H. Thompson, 1915.
Documents inedits.
Vol. 15, pt. 1. Cartulaire de l'Eglise Notre Dame de Paris. ed. Guerard. Paris 1850.
Vol. 12, pt. 1. Cartulaire de l'Abbaye de Saint-Pere de Chartres. ed. Guerard. Paris 1840.
Ducange: Glossarium mediae et infimae Latinitatis. ed. Carpenter & Henschel. Paris 1840.
Ducange: Glossaire Francaise. Paris 1850.
Dugdale, Wm., Monasticon Anglicanum. London 1849.
Liebermann, F., Die Gesetze der Angelsachsen. 2 vols. Halle 1903.
Oliver, George, Monasticon Diocesis Exoniensis. Exeter 1846.
Records of the Borough of Nottingham. Vol. I. London 1882.
"Rolls Series." Chronicles and Memorials of Great Britain and Ireland during the Middle Ages.
Vol. 2, pt. 2. Chronicon Monasterii de Abingdon ed. J. Stevenson.
Vol. 12, pts. 2 (1) and 3. Munimenta Gildhallae Londoniensis. ed. H. T. Riley.
Vol. 28, pts. 4-9. Chronica Monasterii, S. Albani, ed. H. T. Riley.
Vol. 29. Chronicon Abbatiae Eveshamensis. ed. W. D. Macray.
Vol. 31, pt. 2. Year Books of the Reign of Edward I and Edward III. ed. Horwood.
Vol. 43, pt. 3. Chronica Monasterii de Melsa. ed. E. A. Bond.
Vol. 62, pts. 1 and 4. Registrum Palatinum Dunelmense. ed T. D. Hardy.
Vol. 70, pts. 1 and 3. Bracton de Legibus et Consuetudinibus. ed. T. Twiss.
Vol. 72, pt. 2. Registrum Malmesburiense. ed. Brewer & Martin.
Vol. 74. History of the English by Henry Archdeacon of Huntingdon. ed. T. Arnold.

Vol. 79, pts. 1-3. Cartulary of the Abbey of Ramsey. ed. Hart & Lyons.
Vol. 83, Liber benefactorum ecclesiae Ramesiensis. ed. Macray.
Vol. 85, pts. 1-3. Letter Books of the Monastery of Christ Church Canterbury. ed. J. B. Shepherd.
Vol. 96, pts. 1 and 2. Memorials of St. Edmund's Abbey. ed. T. Arnold.
Vol. 98. Records of Parliament 1305. ed. F. W. Maitland.

Royce, D., Landboc sive registrum Monasterii de Winchelcumba. Exeter 1892-1903.

Selden Society.
Vol. 21. Borough Customs, Vol. II. ed. M. Bateson, 1906.

Somerset Record Society.
Vol. 5. Rentalia et Custumaria Monasterii Glastoniae. ed. C. J. Elton, 1891.
Vol. 14. Two Cartularies of the Benedictine Abbeys of Muchelney and Athelney. ed. E. H. Bates, 1899.

Statutes of the Realm. London 1810.

Subsidy Collected in the Diocese of Lincoln, 1526. ed. H. Salter. Oxford 1909.

Surtees Society.
Vol. 83. Cartularium Abbathiae de Rievalle. 1889.
Vol. 89. Cartularium Prioratus de Gyseburne. Vol. II. 1894.
Vol. 130. Memorials of Abbey of St. Mary of Fountains, Vol. III, 1918.

Thorpe, B. Ancient Laws and Institutes of England, 1840.

Wilson, J. M., Worcester Liber Albus. London 1920.

Yorkshire Archaeological Society, Record Series.
Vol. 13. Coucher Books of Selby, Vol. II. ed. J. T. Fowler, 1893.
Vol. 25. Chartulary of St. John of Pontefract, Vol. I. ed. R. Holmes, 1899.
Vol. 30. Chartulary of St. John of Pontefract. Vol. I. ed. R. Holmes, 1902.

Secondary Works

Capes, W. W., English Church in 14 and 15 Centuries. In Stephens and Hunt, History of the English Church, Vol. 3, 1900, pp. 292-294, 303.

Fletcher, J. S., Cistercians in Yorkshire. 1919, pp. 154, 155, 177.

Holdsworth, W. S., History of English Law. 1903.

Pollock, F. and Maitland, F. W., History of English Law before the Time of Edward I., 1908.

Savine, A., English Monasteries on the Eve of Dissolution, in Vol. I, Oxford Studies in Social and Legal History, ed. Paul Vinogradoff, 1909, pp. 240-245.